35 d

SUPER SANDCASTLE™
Let's Learn A to Z

Airedale to Zuchon

Dogs from A to Z

Mary Elizabeth Salzmann

Consulting Editor, Diane Craig, M.A./Reading Specialist

ABDO
Publishing Company

Published by ABDO Publishing Company, 8000 West 78th Street, Edina, Minnesota 55439. Copyright © 2009 by Abdo Consulting Group, Inc. International copyrights reserved in all countries. No part of this book may be reproduced in any form without written permission from the publisher. Super SandCastle™ is a trademark and logo of ABDO Publishing Company.

Printed in the United States.

Editor: Martha E. H. Rustad
Content Developer: Nancy Tuminelly
Cover and Interior Design and Production: Colleen Dolphin, Mighty Media
Photo Credits: Brand X Pictures, Corbis Images, Dag Sundberg/Getty Images, Wegner, P./Peter Arnold, Jess Phillips, Shutterstock, Naomi Simmonds

Library of Congress Cataloging-in-Publication Data

Salzmann, Mary Elizabeth, 1968-
  Airedale to zuchon : dogs from A to Z / Mary Elizabeth Salzmann.
    p. cm. -- (Let's learn A to Z)
  ISBN 978-1-60453-491-7
  1. Dogs--Juvenile literature. 2. English language--Alphabet--Juvenile literature. I. Title.

SF426.5.S237 2009
636.7--dc22

2008023867

Super SandCastle™ books are created by a team of professional educators, reading specialists, and content developers around five essential components— phonemic awareness, phonics, vocabulary, text comprehension, and fluency— to assist young readers as they develop reading skills and strategies and increase their general knowledge. All books are written, reviewed, and leveled for guided reading, early reading intervention, and Accelerated Reader® programs for use in shared, guided, and independent reading and writing activities to support a balanced approach to literacy instruction.

About Super SandCastle™

Bigger Books for Emerging Readers Grades K–4

Created for library, classroom, and at-home use, Super SandCastle™ books support and engage young readers as they develop and build literacy skills and will increase their general knowledge about the world around them. Super SandCastle™ books are part of SandCastle™, the leading preK–3 imprint for emerging and beginning readers. Super SandCastle™ features a larger trim size for more reading fun.

Let Us Know

Super SandCastle™ would like to hear your stories about reading this book. What was your favorite page? Was there something hard that you needed help with? Share the ups and downs of learning to read. We want to hear from you! Send us an e-mail.

sandcastle@abdopublishing.com

Contact us for a complete list of SandCastle™, Super SandCastle™, and other nonfiction and fiction titles from ABDO Publishing Company.

www.abdopublishing.com • 8000 West 78th Street Edina, MN 55439 • 800-800-1312 • 952-831-1632 fax

This fun and informative series employs illustrated definitions to introduce emerging readers to an alphabet of words in various topic areas. Each page combines words with corresponding images and descriptive sentences to encourage learning and knowledge retention. AlphagalorZ inspires young readers to find out more about the subjects that most interest them!

The "Guess what?" feature expands the reading and learning experience by offering additional information and fascinating facts about specific words or concepts. The "More Words" section provides additional related A to Z vocabulary words that develop and increase reading comprehension.

These books are appropriate for library, classroom, and home use.

Aa

Airedale Terrier

Height: 22–24 inches (56-61 cm)
Weight: 45–70 pounds (20-32 kg)

The Airedale Terrier is the largest breed of terrier. U.S. presidents Woodrow Wilson, Warren Harding, and Calvin Coolidge all had Airedales.

Guess what?

The Airedale is known as the King of Terriers.

4

Bb

Guess what.?

Mickey Mouse's dog Pluto is a Bloodhound.

Bloodhound

Height: 23–27 inches (58-69 cm)
Weight: 80–110 pounds (36-50 kg)

The Bloodhound has the best sense of smell of all dog breeds. Bloodhounds are often used by police to find people.

5

Chihuahua

Height: 6–10 inches (15-25 cm)
Weight: 3–10 pounds (1-5 kg)

The Chihuahua is named for the Mexican state where it was discovered. Chihuahuas can be different colors including white, black, and tan.

Guess what?

The Chihuahua is the smallest breed of dog.

Cc

6

Dalmatian

Height: 19–24 inches (48-61 cm)
Weight: 45–70 pounds (20-32 kg)

Dalmatians used to be trained to guard carriages and wagons that were pulled by horses. Dalmatian puppies don't have spots when they are born.

Guess what?

Dalmatians start developing spots when they are about a week old.

7

Dd

English Springer Spaniel

Height: 18–20 inches (46-51 cm)
Weight: 40–55 pounds (18-25 kg)

English Springer Spaniels are often trained to help people hunt birds. They are good swimmers and like to get wet and muddy.

Ee

French Bulldog

Height: 11–13 inches (28-33 cm)
Weight: 19–28 pounds (9-13 kg)

The French Bulldog is a smart, friendly dog. French Bulldogs were bred in France from the English Bulldog, which is bigger.

Ff

Guess what?

A French Bulldog's ears are shaped like bat ears.

Gg

Greyhound

Height: 27–30 inches (69-76 cm)
Weight: 60–70 pounds (27-32 kg)

The Greyhound is the fastest breed of dog. Only a few animals, such as cheetahs and gazelles, can run faster than Greyhounds.

Guess what?

A Greyhound can run up to 45 miles (72 km) per hour.

Havanese

Height: 8–12 inches (20-30 cm)
Weight: 7–13 pounds (3-6 kg)

The Havanese is the national dog of Cuba. Its long fur is very light and provides shade from the sun.

Guess what?

Queen Victoria of England and author Charles Dickens both had Havanese dogs.

Ii

Irish Wolfhound

Height: 28–36 inches (71-91 cm)
Weight: 90–150 pounds (41-68 kg)

The Irish Wolfhound is a very old breed. Hundreds of years ago they were trained to hunt wild boar, elk, and wolves. That is how the breed got its name.

12

Jack Russell Terrier

Height: 10–15 inches (25-38 cm)
Weight: 14–18 pounds (6-8 kg)

Jack Russell Terriers are mostly white, with black or brown markings. They are good jumpers. They can jump as high as five feet (2 m).

Jj

13

Keeshond

Height: 16–19 inches (41-48 cm)
Weight: 35–45 pounds (16-20 kg)

The Keeshond breed
originated in the Arctic.
But it is named for a famous
Dutch man, Kees de Gyselaer.

Guess what?

Keeshond is pronounced
KAYZ-hond.

Kk

14

Guess what?

Most guide dogs in the United States are Labrador Retrievers.

Labrador Retriever

Height: 20–25 inches (51-64 cm)
Weight: 55–80 pounds (25-36 kg)

Labrador Retrievers can be yellow, black, or chocolate. The Labrador Retriever is thought to be the most popular breed of dog in the world.

Ll

15

Mastiff

Height: 27–34 inches (69-86 cm)
Weight: 140–200 pounds (64-91 kg)

The Mastiff is one of the heaviest breeds of dog. Mastiffs are often trained as guard dogs.

Guess what?

The Mastiff is also called the English Mastiff.

Mm

Guess what?

Newfoundlands are often called Newfies for short.

Newfoundland

Height: 25–29 inches (64-74 cm)
Weight: 100–150 pounds (45-68 kg)

Newfoundlands can be black, brown, gray, or black and white. Because they can swim long distances, Newfoundlands are good water rescue dogs.

Oo

Guess what?

Max in *The Little Mermaid* and Barkley on *Sesame Street* are Old English Sheepdogs.

Old English Sheepdog

Height: 21–23 inches (53-58 cm)
Weight: 60–100 pounds (27-45 kg)

Old English Sheepdogs are grey and white. Their long fur helps keep them warm in winter and cool in summer.

18

Pug

Height: 10–14 inches (25-36 cm)
Weight: 13–20 pounds (6-9 kg)

The Pug comes from China and is one of the oldest breeds of dog. Otis in *The Adventures of Milo and Otis* is a Pug.

Guess what?

Pug puppies are sometimes called Puglets.

Pp

Qq

Queensland Heeler

Height: 17–20 inches (43-51 cm)
Weight: 35–50 pounds (16-23 kg)

Queensland Heelers are also called Australian Cattle Dogs or Blue Heelers. They were bred to help ranchers herd cattle.

Guess what?

Queensland Heelers are called heelers because they sometimes nip at the heels of the cattle.

Rhodesian Ridgeback

Height: 24–27 inches (61-69 cm)
Weight: 65–90 pounds (29-41 kg)

The Rhodesian Ridgeback is named for the ridge of fur along its spine. The ridge fur grows in the opposite direction from the rest of the dog's coat.

Guess what?

The Rhodesian Ridgeback was bred in Africa to help people hunt lions.

Rr

Saint Bernard

Height: 25–32 inches (64-81 cm)
Weight: 100–200 pounds (45-91 kg)

The Saint Bernard breed started in Switzerland. They were trained to find and rescue people lost in the Alps.

Guess what?

A Saint Bernard's strong sense of smell helps it find people buried in the snow.

Ss

Toy Poodle

Height: less than 10 inches (25 cm)
Weight: 6–9 pounds (3-4 kg)

Toy Poodles have curly fur that can be cut in different styles called clips. They are the puppy clip, the English saddle clip, the Continental clip, and the sporting clip.

Guess what.?

Poodles were often trained to perform tricks in circuses.

Tt

23

Utonagan

Height: 22–28 inches (56-71 cm)
Weight: 55–85 pounds (25-39 kg)

The Utonagan is a new breed of dog that looks a lot like a wolf. The name Utonagan comes from a Chinook Indian legend and means "Spirit of the Wolf."

Guess what?

Utonagans are bred in England.

Uu

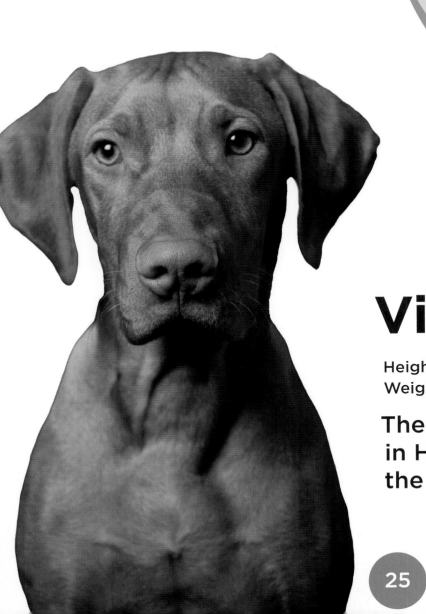

Vv

Guess what?

Vizsla is pronounced *VEEZH-luh*.

Vizsla

Height: 21–25 inches (53-64 cm)
Weight: 40–65 pounds (18-29 kg)

The Vizsla was originally bred in Hungary and is also called the Hungarian Pointer.

25

Ww

Guess what?

Photographer William Wegman takes pictures of Weimaraners dressed up like people.

Weimaraner

Height: 22–28 inches (56-71 cm)
Weight: 55–85 pounds (25-39 kg)

The Weimaraner is a German hunting dog. U.S. president Dwight D. Eisenhower had a Weimaraner.

26

Xoloitzcuintle

Height: 9–24 inches (23-61 cm)
Weight: 5–50 pounds (2-23 kg)

The Xoloitzcuintle is also called the Mexican hairless dog. Its skin is smooth but tough and thick. There is also a coated version of the Xoloitzcuintle that has very short fur.

Guess what?

Xoloitzcuintle is pronounced *show-low-eats-queent-lee.*

27

Yy

Guess what?

Yorkshire Terriers are often called Yorkies.

Yorkshire Terrier

Height: 6–7 inches (15-18 cm)
Weight: 3–7 pounds (1-3 kg)

Yorkshire Terriers have long, silky fur that takes a lot of care. People who don't enter their Yorkshire Terriers in dog shows usually give their dogs short haircuts.

28

Zuchon

Height: less than 13 inches (33 cm)
Weight: 12–14 pounds (5-6 kg)

The Zuchon is a mix of two other dog breeds, the Bichon Frise and the Shih Tzu.

Guess what?

The Zuchon can also be called the Shichon.

Zz

29

Glossary

breed – 1) a group of animals or plants that have ancestors and characteristics in common. 2) to raise animals, such as dogs, that have certain traits.

carriage – a vehicle pulled by horses that people ride in.

develop – to grow or change over time.

distance – the amount of space between two places.

height – how tall something is.

legend – a story about the past that people believe even though it can't be proved.

marking – the usual pattern of color on an animal.

national – of or related to a nation.

originate – to start or begin.

photographer – a person who uses a camera to take pictures.

pronounce – to say correctly.

rancher – a person who raises livestock such as cattle or sheep.

rescue – to save from harm or danger.

ridge – a narrow, raised area on the surface of something.

saddle – the padded leather seat that a horseback rider sits on.

spine – the row of small bones down the middle of a person or animal's back.

tough – strong but flexible.

version – a different form or type from the original.

More Dog Breeds!

Can you learn about these dog breeds too?

Afghan Hound	Collie	Otterhound
Akita	Dachshund	Pekingese
Alaskan Malamute	Doberman Pinscher	Pointer
Basset Hound	English Setter	Pomeranian
Beagle	Fox Terrier	Poodle
Bernese Mountain Dog	German Shepherd	Rottweiler
Bichon Frise	Golden Retriever	Russian Wolfhound
Border Collie	Gordon Setter	Saluki
Borzoi	Great Dane	Samoyed
Boston Terrier	Great Pyrenees	Schnauzer
Boxer	Ibizan Hound	Shar-Pei
Bull Terrier	Irish Setter	Shetland Sheepdog
Bulldog	Japanese Chin	Shih Tzu
Chesapeake Bay Retriever	King Charles Spaniel	Siberian Husky
Chow Chow	Lhasa Apso	Welsh Corgi
Cocker Spaniel	Maltese	Whippet